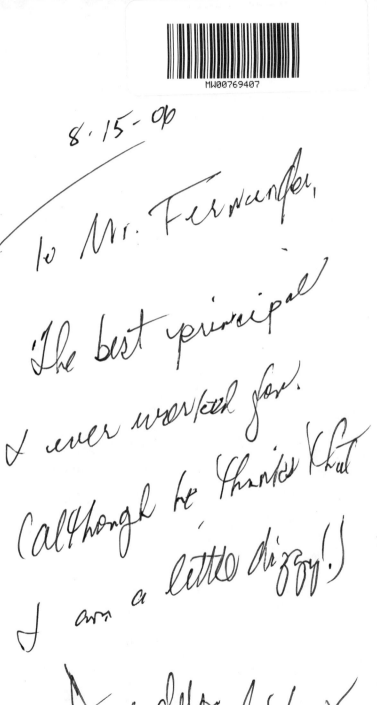

8·15-06

To Mr. Fernandez,

The best principal
I ever worked for.
(Although he thinks that
I am a little dizzy!)

Gwendolyn Cheatham

Give Your Teacher This Note!
(Parents Say the Funniest Things)

by
Gwendolyn Jevita Cheatham, Ph.D.

Bloomington, IN Milton Keynes, UK

authorHOUSE™

AuthorHouse™
1663 Liberty Drive, Suite 200
Bloomington, IN 47403
www.authorhouse.com
Phone: 1-800-839-8640

AuthorHouse™ UK Ltd.
500 Avebury Boulevard
Central Milton Keynes, MK9 2BE
www.authorhouse.co.uk
Phone: 08001974150

First published by AuthorHouse 7/13/2006

ISBN: 1-4208-7287-7 (e)
ISBN: 1-4208-7286-9 (sc)

Library of Congress Control Number: 2005906456

Printed in the United States of America
Bloomington, Indiana

This book is printed on acid-free paper.

Illustrations by Gwendolyn Jevita
Cheatham, Ph.D. and Martin Mensah

With love and affection, I dedicate this publication to my dear mother, Rosanna Manus Cheatham and her twin sister, Georganna Manus Brison *(Auntie Ann)*. These beautiful and courageous women taught me that obstacles are only *temporary* challenges.

Some people were born to dance;
others were born to sing;
I was born to teach.

Acknowledgments

Thanks to my family for their love and encouragement. I thank my friends for awakening in me the desire to publish this collection. I also thank my students' parents for their support throughout the years. Teachers and administrators *need* parents as we attempt to motivate our students to become life-long learners and good citizens.

Give Your Teacher This Note!

Dear teacher,
My daughter says you are *very* smart. I told her that you, *probably*, went to college.

****

Dear teacher,
I visited my child's class. There were 25 students, but only 20 desks were there. Will the students take turns standing, or *what*?

****

Dear teacher,
A mounted police officer caught up with me and gave me a speeding ticket. Do I have to pay it?

****

Dear teacher,
Why do teachers always give homework on Fridays? This messes up the whole weekend.

****

Dear teacher,
I do not know why my child gets such bad grades. His IQ is a perfect *20-20*!

****

Dear teacher,
I will bring my son's project to school later today. His father has not finished it yet.

I am almost finished with my son's project.

Dear teacher,
I have been married to my husband for 25 years. He has been married to me for the *same* amount of time. My 12-year-old son

says we are *too old* to have such a young child. What are our options?

****

Dear teacher,
Our daughter was absent yesterday because she had to take the dog to the *vegetarian*.

****

Dear teacher,
I think computers are taking over the world. E-mail me and tell me what *you* think.

****

Dear teacher,
Do you know where I can find a good tutor? My daughter wants to go to college, and she needs someone to do her homework.

****

Dear teacher,
My daughter is bringing her own water to school because she says the water fountains at the school are broken. Please let her drink it. I do not want her to get thirsty and *dry up*.

****

Dear teacher,
I do not see why my son was suspended for using profanity at school. We use it at home all the time. It is just another foreign language!

****

Dear teacher,
If my son takes Algebra II before he takes Algebra I, do you think he will pass the class?

****

Yes. Most students do take Algebra I before Algebra II.

Dear teacher,
Can animals communicate with one another? I changed my dogs' diet and they appear to be *conspiring* against me.

****

Dear teacher,
Teachers at this school *gives* too much homework. I would like to *learn* my children some things at home, but there *do not be nothing* left to teach them.

****

Dear teacher,
I do not know what the big deal is with cat lovers. We feed them, take care of them, and carry them to the animal doctor. How do they reward us? One night, they let a *burglar* come into our house, steal my husband's most expensive cologne, and then steal *all* of my jewelry. The burglar even fixed himself a *sandwich*. What did the cats do? Nothing! They would not even *bark*.

****

Dear teacher,
My daughter did not start the fight at school, so why was she suspended for beating up the girl who did? You should *reward* her!

****

Dear teacher,
The school is located across the street from a church. I believe this is a conflict between church and state.

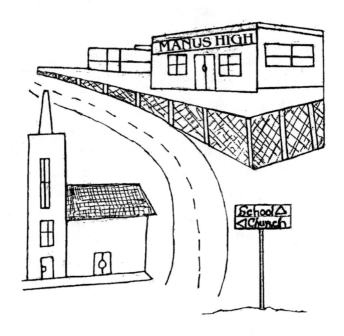

The school is across the street
from the church. Is that o.k.?

Dear teacher,
You teachers have been failing my son since he was in kindergarten. If you keep this up, he will not be able to get into *college*.

****

Dear teacher,
My husband is a blue-collar worker, and he makes more money than teachers do. He is *smarter*, too.

****

Dear teacher,
We are going to the mall a lot during the holiday season. We would like to purchase a gift for you. How *old* are you?

****

Dear teacher,
My wife is a lawyer, so you teachers had better be careful about my son's grades and stuff!

****

Dear teacher,
My daughter thinks she can absorb information by putting her book under

her pillow. Will she need to open the book first?

****

Dear teacher,
My daughter's Prom date backed out. I already bought her dress. Do you know a nice boy who has not asked anyone yet?

****

Dear teacher,
Can you ask the Board of Education to add cooking to the curriculum? My daughter wants to get married someday, and *I* cannot help her.

****

Dear teacher,
My son did not do his homework because an airplane was flying overhead, and he said that he did not hear your directions.

****

Dear teacher,
I do not believe in setting clocks because the noise frightens my children. They might be late to school from time to time.

****

What's wrong with teaching
French cuisine during *history* class?

Dear teacher,
I think you should decorate your classroom
like a French café. If you do this, the children
can get to know the French people.

****

Dear teacher,
My son's clothes do not match because I was in a hurry this morning. Do not let him exchange clothes with anyone.

****

Dear teacher,
My daughter is wearing a brand new diamond ring today. I have not purchased insurance on it yet, so do not tell anyone that it is real.

****

Dear teacher,
Will you please tell my daughter that a screwdriver is a household tool? She thinks it is an alcoholic beverage.

****

Dear teacher,
My children do not like you because you give so much homework. I think you are o. k. (But you *do* give too much homework).

****

The kids hate to leave our beautiful, new house.

Dear teacher,
We recently bought a beautiful, new house and my children love it. Sometimes they are late because they hate to leave home.

****

Dear teacher,
My wife and I argued all night about this politics thing. What is a *shoe-in*? Is it like throwing your hat in the ring?

****

Dear teacher,
Do you have a record of the students who voted in the Homecoming Queen election? I want to collect *every* dollar I gave to the students who did not vote for my daughter.

****

Dear teacher,
My son is only 15 years younger than I am. When I tell him to do his chores at home, he ignores me. Since you are *old*, will you tell him to mind me?

****

Dear teacher,
I think teachers are giving too much homework that requires a computer. They are taking up quality time that children should be spending with their families.

I will expect an e-mail with *your* opinion about this.

****

Dear teacher,
I do not think you should wear so many dark colors. With your complexion, you should wear more pastels. Do not take this personally. It is just a fact. Have a nice day!

****

Dear teacher,
Our boat was stolen. My daughter and I spent the whole week searching for it. She is *extremely* large, and we enjoyed taking her out on the lake.

****

Dear teacher,
Please do not suspend my son from school again. Every time he is suspended, he has a party at our house.

****

Dear teacher,
I do not think my children need to take physical education. They walk at least six blocks to school *everyday*. That should be *enough* exercise.

****

Dear teacher,
You will have to bring my daughter home today. *I* cannot pick her up because *I* have an appointment.

****

Dear teacher,
My daughter is wearing a bra to school for the first time. Make sure that she does not take it *off*.

****

Dear teacher,
I plan to punish my child for acting out at school. He will have to read at least *three* books *this year*.

****

Teachers' Parking Lot

Dear teacher,
Why do teachers drive such old, beat up cars? People will think they do not make enough money to buy a *decent* vehicle.

****

Dear teacher,

If a teacher does not know the subject *he or she* is teaching, could a parent ask the Board of Education to make *him or her* go back to school? (Everyone knows whom I am talking about at that school.)

****

Dear teacher,

I am a single parent with one son and three daughters. Please give my son all male teachers, so he can see what *men* look like.

****

Dear teacher,

I know I promised to volunteer, but I figured the school has enough money to *pay* me.

****

Dear teacher,

Please let my son keep the key to the elevator. The cast is now removed from his leg, but he says he has gotten used to taking the elevator.

****

Dear teachers,
I think teachers should work until at least five o'clock. Parents have a lot of things to do for their families after work.

****

Dear teacher,
Why are you sending me all these notes telling me that my son is a behavior problem? Why do you think I send him to you people everyday?

****

Dear teacher,
Thank you for inviting my daughter to be part of the Magnet Program. My husband and I have a collection of lodestones, if you need them.

****

Dear teacher,
My son received some tokens to ride the bus free. Will he still have to pay?

****

Dear teacher,
I do not have anything against over weight people, but if you lost 20 pounds, you would look a whole lot *better*.

****

Dear teacher,
I think there should be famous paintings in the school. Students can learn their subject matter and art at the same time. They would then learn *double*.

****

Dear teacher,
I am starting a new job Monday. I will not be able to pick up my children from school. What can *you* do about this?

****

Dear teacher,
I do not understand why children cannot wear jeans to the Annual Semi-formal School Dance. They would be more comfortable.

****

Show off!

Dear teacher,
What is the difference between a goose and a duck? I think one of them can fly. Which one is it?

****

19

Dear teacher,

I am sending you some fresh strawberries from our garden. There should be *35* of them. My son *loves* strawberries. Let me know if he eats any of them on the way to school.

****

Dear teacher,

Why can't we have Saturday school? That would give parents *at least one day of freedom* from their children.

****

Dear teacher,

School uniforms would be a great idea. I cannot continue to spend *thousands* of dollars on clothes for my daughters every year.

****

Dear teacher,

Ask the Principal if the children can have brownies everyday. My children love them, but they are too messy to make at home.

****

Dear teacher,

Send me a calendar for the entire school year. I need to set up my hair and nail appointments.

****

Dear teacher,
Will you tell the morning traffic officer at the school to *stay out of the way*? I am always in a hurry, and she makes me late for work.

****

There she is. I am going to be late for work. Again!

Dear teacher,
I hope you enjoyed the flowers I sent your class for Open House. Can you pay half of the cost? My family is on a strict budget. (The bill is attached.)

****

Dear teacher,
I do not mean to hurt your feelings or anything, but purple is *not* your color.

****

Dear teacher,
I apologize for the spot on my son's homework. It was his turn to take out the garbage.

****

Dear teacher,
Please excuse my daughter for being absent *yesterday*. She had Scarlet Fever. Her ears and nose were *extremely* red, so I kept her home. She is over it now.

****

Dear teacher,
I missed the PTA meeting last night. My son's father and I are splitting up, and I thought people would be able to see it on my face.

****

Dear teacher,
Give my son detention today. I need to do some shopping before I pick him up.

****

Dear teacher,
My daughter's homework will be late.
I have not had this course in *years*.

****

Dear teacher,
My son was absent yesterday because he broke the school bully's arm, and wanted to go to the hospital to see it for himself.

****

Oh my! I've got to *defrost* this microwave.

Dear teacher,
Please give my daughter breakfast at school today. When I *defrosted* the microwave this morning, I lost track of the time.

****

Dear teacher,
When I came home yesterday, my son had a girl in his bedroom. Please enroll him in sex education classes *immediately*.

****

Dear teacher,
Is school out in May or June? The family is going on vacation in May, and I need to know if we will have to leave my son at home.

****

Dear teacher,
Would you please tell my son what a *condor* is? I think he is sexually active.

****

Dear teacher,
Everyone knows that Napoleon Bonaparte was married to the Egyptian queen, Cleopatra. Why don't you know that?

****

Dear teacher,
My son and daughter had a big party while my husband and I were out of town. Send me the names and telephone numbers of all their friends. *I want to call their parents* and tell on them.

****

Dear teacher,
Our cat died last night. My son will not come to school tomorrow because his father and I will have to bury him.

****

Dear teacher,
Tell the school's nurse to check the rash on my daughter's arm. If we take her to the doctor, *we* will have to pay.

****

Dear teacher,
Do not give my son milk at school because it gives him a stomachache. (He gets a stomachache when I make him drink it at home, too).

****

Dear teacher,
My daughter is a cheerleader, so do not expect her to do homework on game nights.

****

Dear teacher,
My daughter and I are going shopping after school today. She will be absent tomorrow because she is always exhausted after shopping.

****

It's o.k., mom. I will *walk* the two blocks to the school.

Dear teacher,
My son is late for school everyday because I drop him off two blocks from the school. When I attended that school, I was not a good student. If I drop him off in front of the school, some of the teachers might recognize me.

****

Dear teacher,
My son was absent yesterday because it was a Jewish holiday. We are *Methodist*, but we respect *all* religions.

****

Dear teacher,
My daughter is absent a lot because she does not like school. I dropped out of school, so I do not bother her when she wants to stay home.

****

Dear teacher,
Do not let my daughter smoke at school. She smokes enough at home. Her lungs need to rest while she is at school.

****

Dear teacher,
My husband was sick yesterday, so my daughter stayed home to take care of *me*.

****

Dear teacher,
My children are late today because there was an accident on the expressway. Two *thousand* cars were involved.

Kids, let's tell the teacher that there were 2,000 cars
involved in this accident.

****

Dear teacher,
We *do not* want our son to go on vacation with us this summer. Could he take four classes this semester and the other two classes during summer school?

****

Dear teacher,
My daughter has a terrible cold. Please let her sneeze as much as possible. She needs to blow it out.

****

Dear teacher,
Is this school on the semester system or the quarter system? I think children should go to school more than one-fourth of the year.

****

Dear teacher,
Please let my son take his medication so that he will not have a *fit*, and then have to explain it to you afterwards.

****

Oh, my goodness! Here we go again. Will someone please
teach this boy how to ride a horse?

Dear teacher,
On Monday, my son was riding his horse
and they fell down a hill. He was injured
very badly. We are trying to decide whether
or not to shoot him.

****

Dear teacher,
My son has a weak bladder and has to go to the restroom a lot. Please let him go so he will not *demonstrate* in front of the class.

****

Dear teacher,
My daughter ran away last week. That is why she was absent from school. Now, she is home again. Will you ask her *why* she changed her mind about returning home?

****

Dear teacher,
Some teachers do not know *anything*. Everyone knows that George Washington was the first *Prime Minister* of this country; Abraham Lincoln wrote the Declaration of Independence; and, Thomas Jefferson freed the slaves after Martin Luther King, Jr. put pressure on the country. Teachers should know these *historical facts*.

****

Dear teacher,

Our dog ate the cat's food. My son had to go to the store this morning to get more food. We finally got him to eat. That is why he is late for school.

****

Dear teacher,

I am sorry I do not have time to give more details as to why my daughter is late for school today. I stopped at the pharmacy to get my prescription filled, and I think there was a robbery in progress. Everyone was staring at me real funny like. I got nervous and told the pharmacist that she needed to hurry up. It was *so* quiet in the store. Maybe, it was quiet because it was 7:00 in the morning and everyone was still sleepy. I suppose that if there was a *real* robbery, it will be on the news this evening. Anyway, I hope it was not robbed. That is my favorite pharmacy. I will write you a more *detailed* letter about my child being late when I get home. Ask her for it tomorrow. Thanks!

****

There will be no recess for you today, buddy.

Dear teacher,
My son is upset because my husband and I grounded him. Do not let him do *anything fun* at school today.

****

Dear teacher,
My daughter does not have my permission to smoke at school. If she writes a *fake* note saying that it is from me, please tear it up.

****

Dear teacher,
I fixed my son's lunch today. If he vomits, give him an aspirin and then call me at work.

****

Dear teacher,
My daughter is ill, but I am still sending her to school. I want her to have perfect attendance because this is probably the *only* award she will get on Awards Day.

****

Dear teacher,
My son does not smoke, drink alcohol, or swear. He has never even gotten a speeding ticket. He has only *one* girlfriend, and *always* does his homework. Do you think he is *normal*?

****

Dear teacher,
You might not recognize my daughter, but she is still the *same* person. She just dyed her hair red.

****

Dear teacher,
When school starts, I will be bringing my son back to school. He is looking forward to his *second* year as a senior.

****

There is nothing more fun than
going fishing on a school day.

Dear teacher,
I let my son skip school yesterday because I wanted him to go fishing with me. When I was his age, my father took me fishing during the school day and it was one of the *best* experiences of my life.

****

Dear teacher,
My son drove to school today. He will get his license next week. Please do not tell the school's police officers.

****

Dear teacher,
Our refrigerator stopped working last night. If my daughter's lunch makes her sick, call me immediately.

****

Dear teacher,
My car did not start this morning, so I cannot pick up my children from school. Bring them home at 6:00.

****

Dear teacher,
My boss says I cannot continue to be late for work, but I bring my boys to school before I go to work. Will you ask the Board of Education to change the start time for school?

****

Dear teacher,
My daughter failed all six of her classes. Will she have to go to summer school?

****

Dear teacher,
My daughter does not know the difference between longitude and latitude. Would you explain the difference between long and short to her?

****

Dear teacher,
My son gets sick every morning. Do you think the *teachers* have anything to do with that?

****

What fun. There is no school today.

Dear teacher,
It snowed this week, so I let my children stay home and play in the snow. They made a snowman, and then came inside and had a cup of hot chocolate. It was fabulous! Much better than school.

****

Dear teacher,
My daughter was absent yesterday because we drove by the mall and could not resist going in to shop.

****

Dear teacher,
My daughter says you think she wears her sweaters *too* tight. I know that! She is still growing, and sweaters are expensive.

****

Dear teacher,
Would you please give my son lunch money? We will pay you back *someday*.

****

Dear teacher,
Why do you say my daughter talks too much in class? Children are supposed to talk in class. If children do not talk in class, how will they learn? Talking is a natural thing. Why do you think people have a mouth, if they are not supposed to talk? Her father talks a lot, too. All of us talk at the dinner table. We always let our children talk freely and express themselves. If the teachers at

40

that school do not want my daughter to talk in class, then I will have to consider home schooling her, and she will be able to talk all she wants to.

****

Dear teacher,
My son does not like physical education. He is skinny, and does not want to show his personal parts.

****

Dear teacher,
Why *does* you say my son *have* to stay in school until he *get to be* 16 year old? I was a dropout and I *done* fine.

****

Dear teacher,
Please excuse my son's absence. His horse had a baby, and he wanted to stay home and watch it happen.

****

Dear teacher,
When the school bell rings, it wakes up my baby. Will you tell the principal that it is *perturbing* the whole neighborhood?

****

Dear teacher,
When school is out today, I want you to stand outside with my daughter. I will be there as soon as I can get there. *Do not move.* I do not want to have to look for you.

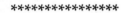

We went to Europe *yesterday* morning, and got back late *last night.*

Dear teacher,
My daughter was absent because we went to Europe yesterday. We returned home very late *last night.*

****

Dear teacher,
My twin daughters were absent because they could not find matching outfits to wear to school. I made them stay home, sort out their clothes, and match them up.

****

Dear teacher,
My children have been late everyday this year because my husband's New Year's resolution is to sleep in an hour later than last year. He is the *only* driver in the house.

****

Dear teacher,
My husband and I did not attend PTA last night because we have one child in elementary school, one in middle school, and another one in high school. We could not make up our minds, so we went to the movies instead.

****

Dear teacher,
On the way to school yesterday, I had a flat tire, the traffic light was stuck, I got a headache, and my youngest child left his

lunch at home. We decided to go back home, eat the lunch, and forget about school.

****

No, no, no. I refuse to stand up when I pledge to the flag.

Dear teacher,
My son does not like to stand for the pledge to the flag. Could he remain seated and pledge to himself?

****

Dear teacher,
I think $5.00 is too much for the PTA dues. That spaghetti dinner was only worth about $2.50.

****

Dear teacher,
Please enter my name as a volunteer at the school. My usual fee for half a day's work is $25.00.

****

Dear teacher,
Did President Jimmy Carter end the Vietnam War? My husband and I had a big discussion about this last night. I said he did. Who is right? Him or me?

****

Dear teacher,
I hope my son's science teacher likes his project. I had to miss work to put it together.

****

Dear teacher,
I missed the PTA meeting. Would you sign my name to the parents' roster? I want to be eligible for the free magazine subscription.

Bye, bye, little froggie.

Dear teacher,
My daughter does not like dead things. Could you ask her biology teacher to let her dissect the frog while it is *still breathing*?

****

Dear teacher,
We are taking our son to Europe with us during the school year. I think he should be counted present because he will be learning a lot of cultural stuff while he is over there.

****

Dear teacher,
The weather channel reported that there would be stormy weather this week. My children are afraid of *torpedoes*, so I kept them home.

****

Dear teacher,
My son lost his driver's license. The school is only a short distance from the house. Could he still drive his car?

****

I miss my little doggie.

Dear teacher,
My husband's precious dog died and this made him very sick. We buried him. That is why my daughter was absent from school yesterday.

****

Dear teacher,
My daughter has an entry in the Science Fair and the Math Fair. Is it too soon to buy a showcase for all the trophies she will win?

****

I'm waiting for another boy to ask me to the dance.

Dear teacher,
My daughter will not attend the school's dance because she does not have a date. Two boys asked her, but she was waiting for one special boy. He did not ask her. Can we get a *refund*?

****

49

Dear teacher,
I think it would be a good idea to plant beautiful, plastic flowers in front of the school. No one would know the difference

****

Dear teacher,
I know that summer school is only for seventh and eighth graders, but I have no summer plans for my sixth grader. Can she attend summer school anyway? This would be a big help to me.

****

Dear teacher,
Isn't it true that President Richard Nixon resigned after the Watergate scandal? Then, President Bill Clinton made him confess to the break-in that took place in Seattle, Washington. I told my husband that this was what happened, but he thinks he knows everything about World War II.

****

Dear teacher,
My son says he does not like the water at school because it is *constaminated*. Can the school do something about this?

****

Dear teacher,
My child is allergic to the plants in your classroom. If you remove them, I will bring you some plastic ones.

****

Dear teacher,
Can my daughter come to school during *Spring Break*? She *needs* to be in school as much as possible.

****

Everyone gets a break, except *me!*

Dear teacher,
My daughter does not like air conditioning because she gets too cold. Please tell the janitor to turn it off in the *entire* school.

****

Dear teacher,
My child hates Mondays. You can expect him to be absent a lot that day of the week.

****

Dear teacher,
Please remove my son from the German class. His grandfather fought in World War I. We lost that war, you know.

****

Dear teacher,
What is the difference between a wrestler and a rassler? We are from Tennessee and we do not wrestle up there, we rassle.

****

Dear teacher,
I do not like the school colors. There is no such thing as a purple and white tiger.

****

Dear teacher,

My husband is a Vietnam veteran. Enroll my son in the high school's *Reserve Officers Training Corps* (ROTC) because I want him to have the same experiences his father had. You understand, don't you?

****

Dear teacher,

My daughter cut her hair. I hate it. Would you *please* tell her that she looks *awful*?

****

Dear teacher,

Can I bring *meat* to the Annual Bake Sale? We have some in our freezer, and we want to get rid of it. (I will cook it first.)

****

Dear teacher,

I want my daughter taken out of the typing class and enrolled in a cooking class. What if she marries a man who likes to *eat*?

****

Dear teacher,

Yesterday, my son beat up the meanest boy in the school. I think he should get recognition for this.

I'm this kid's birthday present.

Dear teacher,
Do you have a place for my son to tie up his horse at the school? He got it for his birthday and wants to ride it to school.

****

Dear teacher,
A teacher told my daughter that she should not drive our new Mercedes to school. I noticed that the teacher's car is an old

jalopy. I think she is jealous. Whose side are you on, the teacher's or mine?

****

Dear teacher,
On Fridays, we like to go to the local seafood restaurant. My children might have to leave school early on those days because the lines are *so long*.

****

Dear teacher,
My son has trouble spelling because he likes to make up his own words.

****

Dear teacher,
My daughter wants to go to Yale University. Her SAT score is *a perfect 500*. I think her chances of getting in are very good, don't you?

****

Dear teacher,
Will you *please* tell my daughter that chocolate milk will not help her get a tan faster?

****

Dear teacher,
Our school mascot is too wimpy. We should change it to something *meaner*.

****

Dear teacher,
Why should I have to pay for the ambulance that transported my child to the hospital? The school called for it, *not me*.

****

Dear teacher,
I think students should sing the school song rap-style, to keep up with the *modern* times.

****

Dear teacher,
My son *does* know the months of the year, just not in the order that *you* want him to know them. What is *wrong* with that?

****

Dear teacher,
My daughter wears blue everyday because that is her favorite color. Why do the children pick on her for not wanting to *mix up* the colors like they do?

****

Dear teacher,
Pretty girls do not have to know as much as boys do. Their husbands will make a living for both of them, won't they?

****

Dear teacher,
If French is a romance language, does that mean that French people are more romantic?

****

Dear teacher,
I was asked to leave the parents' meeting for lighting up a cigarette. My! My! My! Haven't we become bourgeois?

****

Dear teacher,
My daughter does not like to talk in class. Make her ask a lot of questions.

****

Dear teacher,
My son did not complete his English homework because he hates that subject. I

made him spend most of his time on math.
(He *likes* math.)

****

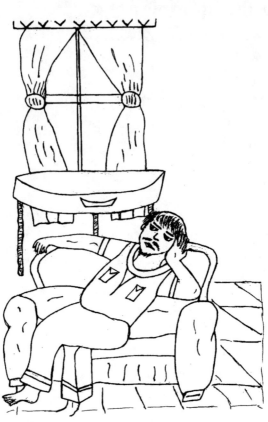

I am such a poor role model for my son.

Dear teacher,
My husband came home intoxicated last
night. My son believes that if his father
could do this, then so could he. If you smell

alcohol on my son's breath, *please* excuse him. He is just trying to be like his father.

****

Dear teacher,
I wrote this note last night. Please excuse me for sending it to you this morning.

****

Dear teacher,
I know you do not know that my husband and I are getting a divorce. My son does not know it yet, either. *Please* do not tell him.

****

Dear teacher,
When my daughter came home today, she had no books. Give her two sets tomorrow.

****

Dear teacher,
It is unfair to ban skateboards from the schoolyard. When the children see the skateboarders coming, they can just *get out of the way!*

****

Dear teacher,
My son is a great football player. I want to know which colleges will be giving him a scholarship.

****

Yea! It's working.

Dear teacher,
My son is not a discipline problem. He was just *testing* the fire extinguisher to see if it was still *working*!

****

Dear teacher,
My child is late because I broke an artificial fingernail and had to fix it this morning. I am getting some real ones tomorrow.

****

Dear teacher,
Our children are late today because we brought them to school in the pickup truck, and had to drive *very* slowly. We did not want to throw them into the traffic. (That might cause an *awful* mess.)

****

Dear teacher,
My son missed the school bus and had to run two blocks to catch up with it. I was *so* proud of him. Track team, look out!

****

Dear teacher,
When my daughter finishes her work at school, she wants to work on crossword puzzles, but *you* want her to go to the technology center in the corner of the room and work *there*. Whose life is it, anyway?

****

Dear teacher,
My son did not do his homework because he was up late last night watching a feature story on television. The title was, "How Homework Helps Students Get Better Grades."

****

Dear teacher,
We are going skiing in February. Give my son *all* of his homework in *January*.

****

Dear teacher,
When my daughter tried to do her homework, *I* did not understand it. So, I told her that she did not have to do it.

****

Dear teacher,
My son is wearing a suit to school today because he said he wanted to dress up. Please do not make him *take it off.*
(Thank you.)

Dear teacher,
My husband traded in the family car for a new truck. It has only two seats. Now, the children will have to walk to school. They will probably be late a lot.

****

Dear teacher,
I bought my three boys the same shoes, but in different colors: black, brown, and blue. This morning, they got the shoes mixed up. I pulled over to the side of the road so they could match them up. I wanted them to have the *same colors on each foot*. You understand, don't you?

****

Dear teacher,
I spanked my son this morning because he would not eat his breakfast. I am sorry he is late. Next time, I will spank him the night before.

****

Dear teacher,
My children do not like school lunches, so I make their lunches every morning. This takes *a lot of time*, you know.

****

Dear teacher,
I have *never* been to a PTA meeting. Do people dress up, or can I wear *just any old thing?*

****

Dear teacher,
On the way to school yesterday, I ran out of gas. Today, I stopped at the gas station twice. (I did not want to run out *again.*)

****

Getting my family ready for work and school is a *big* job!

Dear teacher,
When you have three boys, two girls, a husband, two dogs, and a cat, it is hard to feed them, dress them, and get out of the house on time. (Oh! I forgot *myself*.)

****

Dear teacher,
Please let my daughter eat the lunch she brings from home. She refuses to eat school lunches.
****

Dear teacher,
Yesterday, I was sick, my son was sick, and my husband was sick, too. Can you fax him his homework? I do not want him to get behind.

****

Dear teacher,
My son is enrolled in summer school. Will he have to go to school on the Fourth of July?
****

Dear teacher,
My son says he likes you better than his other teachers. Tell him to stop ditching his other classes.

****

Dear teacher,
What time does the school day end? When I get there at 5:00, no one is there but *my* children.

****

Dear teacher,
Can my son bring his dog to school? He is not *blind*. The dog is not housebroken, and I do not want him to mess up *our* house.

****

Dear teacher,
My family is visiting us next week. We have not seen them in years. I will send my children back to school when they leave.

****

Dear teacher,
After the big rainstorm yesterday, *our* lights went out. I kept my daughter home because she does not like the dark.

****

Dear teacher,
My daughter is bringing her Prom dress to school to show her friends. I hope it is o.k.

****

Dear teacher,
I think my son should get a trophy in football. I *know* he played basketball this year, but he played football last year.

****

Dear teacher,
My son said his teacher took his class *outside* during the tornado drill. Do the teachers normally do *that*?

Are we supposed to go *outside* during a tornado drill?

Dear teacher,
My daughter is wearing her brother's shoes to school because her shoes do not fit. Her feet grow *so* fast.

****

Dear teacher,
Please take brownies off the Bake Sale list. I am allergic to chocolate.

****

Dear teacher,
What is wrong with my son coming to school barefoot? He hates shoes. We even let him go barefoot when he wears his suits to *church*.

****

Dear teacher,
Can my daughter go to the front of the lunch line? I know this might sound selfish, but she gets bored just standing there, *waiting*.

****

Dear teacher,
My child was not enrolled in school for the past year, but our entire family is going on vacation for the next three months, and we want him enrolled in a school before we leave.

****

Dear teacher,
Could the Board of Education paint the buses another color? Yellow is *so* ugly.

****

Dear teacher,
My family wants to invite you to dinner. Are you Jewish, Christian, or what? We do not want to prepare the *wrong* food.

****

Dear teacher,
Our children are caught in the middle of a bad marriage. Do not say we should get a divorce. *We tried that*! It did not work, so we got married again.

****

Dear teacher,
I want my son's French class changed to Spanish because the French people smoke *too* much.

****

Does a tree grow from the *trunk* or the top of the *branches?*

Dear teacher,
Do trees grow from the branches or the trunks? I cannot see all the way to the top, but I can see the bottom of the tree. The trunks always look the *same* to me.

****

70

Dear teacher,
Stop giving my son so much work that requires the Internet. We *do not* have a computer. If you want him to have a computer, you can just go to the computer store and *buy him one*!

****

Dear teacher,
Students should stand up and stretch every five minutes or so. This will keep the blood flowing to their brains, and then they will not forget everything they *do not want* to remember.

****

Dear teacher,
Do you wear a wig, or is that your real hair? If it *is* your real hair, then it is very pretty. If *not*, well, you know.

****

Dear teacher,
I do not believe teachers should show videos at school. This wastes time. I can take my children to the movies myself. The principal should make the teachers use only *books*!

Dear teacher,
Men who teach the *same* subjects as women should be expected to know as much about the subject as women do. Why do some of them get away with *half knowledge*?

****

Dear teacher,
I pay taxes! Schools should provide students with pencils, paper, and everything else they need. If they cannot do that, I want a complete *outline list* of everything the schools are doing with all that education tax money I pay every year!

****

Dear teacher,
At the beginning of the school year, parents should meet with the Board of Education and tell them what the children should have for lunch. Most of the food is *high-caloried*.

****

Dear teacher,
I noticed that the boys' restroom is directly across the hall from the girls' restroom.

What if they *get them mixed up* someday and end up in the wrong restroom? Then, what will happen? *Huh*?!

****

Dear teacher,
My son has worn eyeglasses all of his life. Now, he wants to get *contact lenses*. Do you think he will read as well as before?
I think he should stick with the eyeglasses. (His reading is nothing to *brag* about, anyway.)

Parents say the funniest things.

Printed in the United States
55974LVS00001B/448-549

9 781420 872866